A FRANK TALK ON

DIVORCE

Could We Have Misunderstood What Jesus Said?

BY FRANK FRIEDMANN

Copyright © 2015, 2016
by Frank Friedmann
All rights reserved.
2nd edition.

ISBN 978-1533360052

Published by Joshua Gordon BookWorks

www.joshuagordonbookworks.com

"This little book is life changing! Frank has addressed the area that historically has been addressed without reference to the tender love and grace of God. Because of this, vast numbers of believers are living out their lives in guilt, shame and hopelessness. You will find here a balanced exegesis of a very difficult subject that allows the light of the vastness of God's love to be seen in a fresh and new way. This is a must read for everyone who has been or is in the middle of divorce. These truths are imperative for all who counsel those whose lives have been broken by divorce. Thank you Frank for a fresh wind of grace in an area that historically has been left to the poisonous air of despair and shame."
- Malcolm Smith, author, speaker, teacher

"Concise, solid, and Biblical. Full of grace that is truthful and truth that is gracious. No matter where you may stand on this issue of divorce and remarriage in the church you will want to consider this well reasoned position before you prayerfully draw your own conclusions."
- Steve Pettit, pastor and director of One in Christ Ministries

"Pastor Frank Friedmann has done his due diligence in exegeting the inspired scriptures to determine what God has really said about divorce and remarriage. In putting his observations into written form in this book, Frank has done a real service to God's people in a way that will minister to those who have experienced divorce, to those who are considering divorce, and to those who simply want to understand God's mind in this matter. This book deserves to be read by God's people."
- Jim Fowler

CONTENTS

Foreword by Preston Gillham • **7**

You Are Not a Disappointment • **13**

Divorce Is Meant to Protect • **17**

Could the Church Be Missing Something? • **27**

The Critical Greek Translation Error • **37**

Jesus Condemned Abandonment, Not Divorce • **41**

"God Hates Divorce" Doesn't Mean What You Think It Does • **47**

God Himself Is a Divorcee • **49**

A Note to Church Leaders • **57**

A Note to Readers Considering Divorce • **59**

A Note to Divorced Readers • **61**

Acknowledgements • **63**

FOREWORD BY PRESTON GILLHAM

On the day she graduated from nursing school, which was also her birthday and our fifth anniversary, my wife walked away from our marriage and didn't come back. She gave no warning, no clues, and no explanation beyond, "I don't love you."

That was nearly thirty years ago and this is the first time I've put my experience in a published writing. Divorce. Two is equally divided—but marriage is not two. Marriage is a covenant that unites two into one, and one is not divisible. In order to separate one, you must tear it apart.

My world collapsed and I collapsed in after it. I retreated to the woods and rivers for consolation. Daily I buried my face in my dog's fur for warmth and the affection of a heartbeat that wouldn't leave me. Yes, of course I leaned upon God. I'm no fool. I cried out to Him and He comforted me, just as He promised. There were many comforts in retrospect, but chief among them early on were the rhythmic swish of my fly rod and the deep darkness of woods long after the sun set. How many nights did I sit engulfed in the night sounds with my dog? I don't know, but for many months it was every night.

I knew my career as a professional minister was over. The decision to immediately cancel all of my engagements was self-evident. It was the right and responsible thing for me to do professionally. What church or conference center wants a minister whose wife has left? It didn't matter that I didn't have a clue why she left or that I was scrambling to fix the situation. What mattered was that she was gone.

What caught me by surprise was my church—the people who knew me, loved me, trusted me, and greeted me each time the doors were open. They were well acquainted with me and far too familiar with me to miss anything that might justify a wife's exit. Initially, I hid from them to protect my wife and make it as easy as possible for her to return. They wouldn't miss me. They would assume I was on the road, not languishing in utter distress beside some river. But when it was no longer possible to hide the reality that I was alone in my house, I turned to them a broken, bereft, disoriented, and rejected husband.

They shunned me. Removed me. Assumed evil about me and justified their separation with selections from the Bible. My best friend led the way. Without asking a single question about what transpired, I was declared unfit and unwelcome by my friend, the church, its leadership, and the church staff.

Reputed to be safe, populated by people of grace and mercy, the church proved the greatest trial and tribulation for me as I sorted through my grief—and they remained such for the duration of my ordeal. While invoking the name of God and allegiance to Scripture, my Christian community afflicted upon me a similar rejection to that of my departed wife.

As Scripture declares, God is faithful. His mercies are new every morning and His lovingkindness is everlasting. My heavenly Father began to reassemble my world, but at almost every turn He did so over the impediments of those declaring His name who thought they were defending His standard.

After a number of years, I remarried. Dianne and I celebrated our twenty-fifth anniversary last summer. Our lives and marriage are full and fulfilled. We have personal and marital walks with Father God that anchor us, guide us, and bring consistent joy to us. We married each other confident that our marriage was blessed by God and biblically approved. We also married with groomsmen and ushers instructed (by me) to forcibly remove anyone from the ceremony who dared disrupt our marriage on convictions of shame that we were entering into an adulterous relationship because I had been married once before.

Divorce is devastating regardless of what precipitates it. There is no such thing as a good divorce. No matter how dysfunctional a marriage might be, marriage is by definition the merging of two into one. Divorce is the tearing apart of that oneness leaving two people with ragged wounds and tender, ugly scars.

Remarriage is not for the faint of heart. Never mind for the moment the contents of the book you are about to read. Entering back into marriage after a divorce is a dicey proposition.

Divorce afflicts about half the population. Is remarriage forbidden? Is half the population living in adultery? Are Dianne and I living in sin because we are married? Was my church justified in treating me as an outcast, one fallen from grace, because my wife divorced me? Is the Bible definitive on this subject, and if so, are we certain of what it says? Can we be certain? The default answer is, yes. The Bible is declarative and clear: Remarriage is forbidden except by narrow definition.

This position feels justified for those governing the world by rules, especially rules that appear biblical. But for those engaging with life, divorce and remarriage cry out for more clarity than tradition, default, and isolated Bible verses. Without compromising Scripture or being soft on the covenant of marriage, is there biblical counsel—sound, exegetical, conservative counsel from God's Word—that should guide us through the morass of a marriage gone awry and a determination to try again?

I have known Frank Friedmann for a long time—well over two decades. Frank is above all honest, but he is also a man of tremendous heart. It is this blend in my friend that has compelled him to look carefully at Scripture concerning divorce and remarriage while capturing in its pages the mercy of God. Although Frank is proficient in the original languages of the Bible, and utilized his expertise to compose this book, he presents his findings in sufficient clarity and simplicity that you can look for yourself into Scripture and the heart of God.

Do this. Look. Examine the Scriptures. Vow to be noble-minded regarding God's inspiration as those were who are mentioned in Acts 17:11. Ask the Holy Spirit for guidance as you read. Let Frank's writing guide you, but rely upon Scripture and the counsel of the Spirit to bring you to a conclusion. The subject of divorce and remarriage is too important and too pervasive to base your position on emotion, tradition, or church standard.

I recommend Frank's study, scholarship, conclusions, accountability, and book to you. I would not have written this foreword nor would I have chosen this forum to reveal my story if I didn't.

Preston Gillham
Fort Worth, Texas
March 2016

YOU ARE NOT A DISAPPOINTMENT

If you're reading this book right now, I assume you are either divorced or are anticipating a divorce. I assume you are hurting right now, that you might even describe what's going on in your soul as desperate. Ominous waves of guilt and shame, failure and loss seem to pound you every day and you've picked up this little book to see if there might be some answer for you, some semblance of hope that what you feel right now is not the final word on your situation. I am also going to assume that fear is your companion, fear that as you read you'll find the judgement and condemnation you have found so often when anyone related to the church addresses this issue of DIVORCE!

Yes, for you it's been the role of "second-class citizen" in the local church. You have a stigma, a black cloud that hangs over you, the type you often see in comic strips. However, this is no cartoon and the black cloud is very real. Perhaps you've been told you cannot teach Sunday School, or that you can never serve in a leadership role, or even worse that you cannot ever receive the Lord's table because you are one of *those* people! YOU ARE DIVORCED! Isn't that how it's often presented by those who represent God? And isn't that presentation a confirmation of the raging guilt and persistent shame that are screaming inside you? Indeed, the church has confirmed the judgement on you that you yourself proclaimed, "I have failed God! I have failed my family! I have failed the church!" And now your conviction is that divorce is indeed, at least practically if not in actuality, the unforgivable sin!

But what if the church, my friend, didn't get this one right? After all, the church is made up of fallible men who don't always interpret and apply the Bible correctly! The church in its history sold the forgiveness of God in a system called indulgences. The church burned people alive at the stake for theological differences. The church killed Jewish people in the name of Jesus! We, the church, have a checkered past when it comes to how we've interpreted and implemented what Father God has taught us in his Word.

I say this, not to undermine the church or our Bible translations in any way, but to call all of us to be like the noble Bereans of Acts 17. In that chapter, Paul called the Christians in Berea "more noble than any other people" because they did not immediately receive what Paul told them about God. Instead, they went home and searched the Scriptures thoroughly to see if what Paul was saying was true.

Now please hear me, I am not "dissing" the church. You and me, we are the church and it would be foolish to "diss" ourselves. But, as I said earlier, the church is people, and we as people don't always get it right. And when we're wrong, we need to be corrected and trained in what is right and true.

That's the journey I am asking you to go on in this little book. I want you to be a Berean and search the Scriptures with me and see if we might have missed what God intended concerning divorce and remarriage. Let's you and I see if Jesus really said what we think He said, and if we missed it, let's admit that we missed it and start presenting the issue the way Jesus Himself presented it. I would remind you as we begin, that the heart behind everything Jesus did and said was to bring freedom from bondage and lies, as He establishes men and women in the truth that sets them free!

Dear Father, this has been a very difficult issue for so many. You intended marriage to be such a blessing for us. But because sin has entered the world, and there is an enemy who seeks to steal, kill, and destroy that source of blessing has instead become a source of such great sorrow and hurt. Father, sometimes that hurt and sorrow are so great, we end up with our hope shattered beyond repair. We see divorce as the only way for us and our children to survive. But now what? Is there forgiveness for us who have broken our marriage vows? Is there the potential for such restoration that we could indeed have a second chance at marriage? Father, is your grace sufficient for such a one to again be a full citizen with full rights in the assembly of the saints to even attain leadership in the church again? These are the questions we need answers for. So Father, as we study your written Word, may your Holy Spirit enlighten our hearts as we seek the truth that brings peace, freedom, and joy to our lives. In Jesus' name, amen!

2

DIVORCE IS MEANT TO PROTECT

I've been a Christian for a long time now, and a pastor for what often seems like a longer time. I went to a very good conservative evangelical seminary. I've spent many years under gifted Bible teachers and scholars who I love, respect, and hold in the highest regard to this day. All through these years of study, I've found the church has a consistent answer for whether or not a Christian can divorce and remarry. They herald, as well we should, that when God designed marriage for man and woman, He designed that they marry for life. This intention is made very clear in the 19th chapter of Matthew. There Jesus states explicitly when a man and a woman join themselves together in marriage they become one flesh. To make this crystal clear, Jesus added that they are no longer two separate people. God views marriage as an actually occurring transformational "oneness" that is never to be broken. Jesus proclaimed authoritatively in this passage, "What God therefore, has joined together let no one ever separate."

Father God has affirmed conclusively that He intended marriage to last a lifetime. Then why, my friends, did God through Moses "command" that men give their wives a certificate of divorce when their marriage falls apart? This is the same question the Pharisees had when Jesus dealt with this issue of marriage being for life. Jesus responded that it was because of the hardness of man's heart that God "commanded" divorce. Now, did you notice that I put the word "commanded" in quotes? That is because that word "commanded" is going to be very important later in our discussion. Now stop for a minute and ponder this declaration from God's inspired Word. God Himself actually COMMANDED divorce in His Word, even though Jesus Himself, Who is God the Son, declared that divorce is something that humanity was never intended to experience. How are we to reconcile those two authoritative statements? That provides us with a difficulty that many in the church have refused to address. I promise you we will address it here—LATER. For now, I want you to focus on the words that follow the command to divorce... Jesus then said these key words, "... but from the beginning it was not so" (Matthew 19:18).

Did you hear those words? They are very important, foundational words for this study. "From the beginning, it was not so." When we come to the issue of divorce we need to understand that divorce is something that we were never intended to experience. We need to agree on this one because God Himself said it is so. But let's have some biblical integrity here and interpret this truth in light of the rest of the scriptures. It is true that we were never intended to experience divorce, but in the same way we were never intended to experience what it was like to lie, to steal, to lust, or to rage. From the beginning, God intended us to live life in purity and innocence in the Garden of Eden. My friends, if you had not recognized it yet, THIS IS NOT THE GARDEN OF EDEN ANYMORE. We no longer live the way God designed us to live in any arena of our lives. Through our own choices and the choices others make, we experience things we were never designed to experience. So let's be honest and admit that divorce is just one of those common things that humanity experiences that were never God's intended experiences for us. Now, if that's true, then why is forgiveness and restoration offered for those who lie, steal, and even murder, but there is very little forgiveness and restoration offered for those who divorce?

In Proverbs 6, the Holy Spirit declares there are seven things God hates: a proud look, a lying tongue, hands that shed innocent blood, a heart that devises wicked imaginations, feet that are swift in running to mischief, a false witness that speaks lies, and he that sows discord among brethren. Did you see it? Or perhaps I should ask did you not see it? If ever God had an opportunity to declare what He hates, it's here and yet, divorce is NOT on that list.

Now some would be quick to point out that in Malachi 2 it says "God hates divorce!" But is that really what God says? Again, we will have more to say on that verse later. For now, though, let's focus on what is found on that list. We find "a proud look, and an arrogant spirit." This is the only thing that's repeated on that list of things God hates, and He stated it in two different ways just to make sure we got it. The supreme thing God stands against is pride or arrogance. Sadly, in my years of ministry, I've seen these two hated attributes reign when it comes to those who've been divorced. Those who have not been divorced display a very negative and haughty attitude toward those who have been divorced, and mark it well my friend, God hates, clearly and obviously hates, that proud and arrogant spirit, of this we can be certain.

Some at this point in their reading might be led to say that I have a very low view of marriage. Let me assure you that nothing could be further from the truth. The New Testament heralds loudly and firmly that God holds marriage in very high regard. Marriage carries a special significance because it provides us the opportunity to give the world a visible, physical picture of the love of Jesus for His church. In the New Testament, Jesus calls Himself the groom, and He calls the church, His bride. He laid down His life for the church, to win her and purify her, so He could present her spotless. The church, His bride, in turn, lays down her life for Him, to serve Him and love Him. A true Spirit-led marriage provides us the opportunity to preach this glorious good news without saying a word by simply dramatizing the Gospel as we live our roles in the marriage union. A Christian man has the opportunity to lay down his life for his bride, and provide the world with a visible demonstration of the love of God. A Christian woman has the opportunity to be devoted to and honor her husband, vividly and powerfully demonstrating to the world the transformational love that takes place when a bride receives such unconditional love. Christian marriage, lived out in obedience to our Father's Word, through the power of the Holy Spirit living in and through us, provides us with the opportunity to dramatize the Gospel!

Did you notice the key word in the last paragraph—opportunity? I highlight that word because that's all it is. It's an opportunity that comes with no guarantee! Marriage requires choice on the part of each individual to live in obedience to God through a dependence on the Holy Spirit. No one on this planet does that perfectly, NOT EVEN CLOSE! Marriage thus also provides us with more than ample opportunity to wound each other, disappoint, and frustrate each other. And let's be honest, marriage provides us with a huge opportunity to devastate each other. Because of our fall into sin, there are a myriad of choices available for us to choose other than love! At any given moment, either of us involved in this union called marriage, can make the choice or take the opportunity to be harsh, selfish, hurtful, or deceitful. We can choose to lie, manipulate, control, cheat, deceive, or reject our spouse in any given breath we take on this planet. Sadly, all of us choose to take advantage of these sinful opportunities all too often in our lives. Sometimes in an instant, more often over time, by making these simple, sinful choices we erode our marriages like the weather erodes the surface of our planet. Like the relentless pounding of the waves breaks down our shoreline and turns it into sand, our marriages get pummelled by sin until sand is all that's left of the once dearly-held foundation of love between us.

I wish we lived in a world untainted by sin. I lie awake at times and dream of what life could be like, or maybe better, what life used to be like in the glory of Eden. In the morning though, I wake up and as I experience the day, the reality of a fallen world aggressively confronts me. As I interact with the people around me I realize that life on this planet is not being experienced as God intended for it to be experienced. We need to be honest about this. There's very little on this planet that we experience on a daily basis that was experienced by Adam and Eve in the Garden of Eden. Oh to be sure, we can experience Eden through the intimate life we share with God, and we can experience life from the church that has God dwelling in and through them, but there is very little in this fallen world that resembles Eden. The result of course, is that things happen in this world. Bad things! One of those bad things is divorce. Father knows that and has addressed what to do about it in His Word.

The great glory of the New Testament is that our Father made a choice before time even began to accomplish a work that would assure that the bad we experience would not be the end of the story. We have a God who is so big, and so strong, and so holy, and so full of love, that He can overcome wrong and make it right. He declares in His Word that He can bring beauty out of ashes, and restore the years that the locusts have eaten. Over the centuries since the death and resurrection of Jesus Christ, this has been the experience of those who have placed their faith in Christ. Despite wrong choices, hurtful, damaging experiences, countless ordinary people have found joy, peace, forgiveness, and restoration through the person and work of the Lord Jesus Christ. Murderers, liars, adulterers, and thieves have had their lives radically transformed through their faith in Christ. Many of these former sinners, now made saints, have gone on to become pastors and missionaries. In the Bible itself, some of the worst sinners even became apostles. This is how great the finished work of Christ is. Bad things happen, we can all attest to that. The glory of the gospel is that God can take those bad things and make them good. How is divorce an exception to that rule?

Sadly, though, at least in my experience, divorce has been treated as the exception to the rule by much of the church. Throughout the history of the church it's been declared that any sin can be repented of and restoration made possible except for divorce. As I've served Christ these many years and shared in the lives of so many the forgiveness and restoration of Christ in their lives, this has been the experience of far too many believers. Liars, thieves, and even adulterers, and murderers have been restored in the churches they've attended, but the divorced have been shunned and ostracized.

Most of these people have shared with me that according to their understanding of Father's Word, there were only two circumstances in which a believer may divorce and be remarried. If divorce occurred apart from those two special circumstances, then the divorce occurred apart from biblical grounds. This means accordingly, that God does not accept the divorce and neither should the church. No matter what the spiritual background of the individuals, be they Methodist, Baptist, Presbyterian, or Pentecostal, this has been their common understanding. I must admit, that I too once held to this understanding. It was what I was taught, and it appeared to be what Father was saying in His Word. In the next chapter, we'll investigate this interpretation and understanding and see if that is what God really said in His Word.

Father, we affirm your Word, that when men come to know the truth, that the truth shall make them free. But Father, the flip side is equally true. If men believe lies, then they will be bound. Father, there have been many lies told in church, and there is much bondage resulting from those lies. As we search out your Word, may your Spirit enlighten our understanding that we might see and embrace the truth, and experience the freedom that you intend for us to experience as your children who walk in the light of your love and grace. Father, we believe that your grace is available to every child of God, that no sin can ever be committed that is bigger than the Life of Jesus that was offered on our behalf on the cross... and that includes grace for the divorced!

3

COULD THE CHURCH BE MISSING SOMETHING?

We saw in the last chapter that God holds marriage in the highest regard and that He intended marriage to be for life. We live, however, in a fallen world, enduring an evil onslaught against us as we seek to shine the light of God in a very dark world that seeks to snuff out our light. As the world, the enemy, and the power of sin hurl themselves against us, we very often make bad choices, and bad choices turn the joy of marital bliss into marital hell. Very often, sinful choices made by us, and by our spouse, can destroy our union. Is there an escape clause to the vows we made? Is there a way out of the hell we are experiencing? Can a believer divorce their spouse and remarry another person? Does God in His marvelous grace ever sanction divorce and remarriage?

There are many varied opinions on this issue in the multitude of books that have been written. However, we as believers are called to seek the revealed Word of God—not human opinion. In searching out in Father's Word there is one clear circumstance which not only allows for, but actually encourages the believer not only to divorce, but to also remarry. The support for this is found in I Corinthians 7. In this section, Paul is answering specific questions that the Corinthians had asked him in a letter they had previously written to him.

In I Corinthians 7, Paul affirmed that if a believer is married to an unbeliever, and the unbeliever does not want to be married to the believer any longer, the believer is to let the unbeliever leave. The tense of the verb is very strong, indicating a command to let them go. Paul made it clear that the believer is not to fight for the marriage and in fact, not even contest the divorce! Paul, inspired by the Holy Spirit, declared that such a believer is called to peace. The strong implication is that there is no guilt or shame to be levied on the believer as a result of the departure of the unbelieving spouse, and that would logically imply that the now divorced believer is free to remarry. God made it very clear that His children were not to be in bondage for the rest of their lives to someone that He Himself did not have a relationship with. So here we have a very clear allowance for divorce in the Scriptures.

Let's turn our attention to what many in the church believe is a second situation in which God allows for divorce and remarriage. Jesus states very clearly in Matthew 5:32 that if a spouse commits adultery divorce is allowed. When a person commits adultery they have already broken the marriage covenant and the right of the offended spouse is protected by God allowing the dissolution of the marriage. But keep in mind here that the key word is "allowed." Remember, God is and always will be about forgiveness and restoration as the ideal, even when adultery has occurred. Nevertheless, God allows divorce when the sin of adultery has occurred in a marriage. So there you have it, God allows divorce for two reasons. One, if a believer is married to an unbeliever and the unbeliever chooses to leave the marriage, and two, if a spouse commits adultery. This has been the predominant teaching in the church for centuries.

We must ask though if this teaching is biblically correct. What if you are married to somebody who is physically abusive and beating the daylights out of you every day? Well, the church has said, "You can separate and you can even divorce but you cannot remarry because Jesus said, divorce is only allowed for adultery"! I struggle with that. Do you struggle with it? So if that's the case, are you telling me that the innocent party is sentenced to a life of singleness because they have an abusive spouse? Are you telling me that the innocent party is sentenced to a life of burning with God given sexual passion that will go unfulfilled because of their sinning spouse? What about the charge from God in I Corinthians 7 that a person who has that passion should get married; does that not apply to a divorced person? Can't you see that this is telling these divorced people they cannot function as the human being God created them to be? Now I ask you, does that sound like God to you? Is that in harmony with His character as revealed in the person of Jesus?

Let's dig a little deeper. What if that spouse is emotionally abusive and speaking death in their tongue to you every day of your life? (Proverbs 18:21). What if your spouse refuses to express the sexual union with you? What if the spouse in their parenting is provoking your children to wrath? What if every day of life in your home your spouse is destroying your children with "death words?" ("You stupid idiot! I don't know why we ever had you! You are such a disappointment to your mother and me. We would be so much better off without you.") And what if that spouse refuses to dialogue or seek counsel to change the way they're living? What if the spouse is addicted to drugs and alcohol? What if the spouse refuses to work and support their family? What if the spouse is a workaholic and is NEVER home, failing to express the life and love of Christ to their spouse and children? Have not those spouses already broken their marriage covenant to love, honor, and cherish? Is there still even a marriage at that point?

One writer, and he's not alone, says these words, "These are hard truths but there are only two reasons given in scripture that allow for divorce and remarriage. One is if the unbeliever leaves, two is if there has been adultery. THERE ARE NO OTHER EXCEPTIONS. REMARRIAGE IS STRICTLY

FORBIDDEN FOR ANY OTHER REASON!" If I shared this leader's name with you, you would know him; and again, he is not alone. This is the standard view in Christendom today. Let me quote for you another internationally known Bible teacher who I will keep nameless. "If a Christian does divorce another Christian except for adultery, neither person is free to marry another. They must stay single or rejoin their former mate. In God's eyes, that union has never been broken. These are not a counselor's suggestions but the Lord's commands."

When I read that, I say, "REALLY?" Does that sound like God, who has revealed himself in the person of Jesus Christ—the one from whom we have received grace upon grace?

NEITHER PARTNER IS FREE TO MARRY ANOTHER? Does that sound like grace? Does this sound like the God of the second chance, of new beginnings? The God who makes all things new?

What if that partner didn't want the divorce? What if that partner who did want the divorce goes out and marries somebody else? Is the innocent party still unable to remarry?

All too often, Christian leaders respond unequivocally: the divorced spouse must remain single. After all, how do we know that the sinning spouse might not repent someday and restore the marriage? REALLY? An innocent party is sentenced by God to a life of singleness because of the sinful behavior of another? The church says, "Yes" to those questions.

Jesus Himself stated it clearly in Matthew 5:32, "Every one of you who divorces his wife except for the cause of immorality makes her commit adultery and whoever marries a divorced woman commits adultery." Let's you and I agree those are really, really strong words from Jesus, that seem to leave little room for alternate interpretations. Let me quote for you from another prominent voice commenting on this passage: "God's desire is that a man and a woman should live together as the marriage vows put it—for better or for worse until death do us part! Wives are not to leave their husbands, difficult as a marriage may become. Husbands are not to divorce their wives even if they appear to be almost irreconcilably incompatible." This is not a passage that needs debate. He makes it crystal clear, it is not in doubt in the least degree. "Even if a spouse gains a divorce, they are to remain single or reconcile because in God's sight the marriage is not broken."

Statements such as these are quite typical of the church, both historically and into the present day. If you have been in church for any length of time you have encountered it. I know this because I, myself, have heard it. Does this echo the Father's heart? Does this sound like the God who has revealed Himself in the person of Jesus Christ—the one from whom we have received grace upon grace?

COULD WE HAVE MISUNDERSTOOD WHAT JESUS SAID?   33

"If a believer marries a person who has divorced their spouse for any reason other than the two exceptions given in scripture, they will live their married life in a perpetual state of adultery. Now God is going to forgive them, but they will live in a perpetual state of adultery."

Now, some in the church will be a little more gracious:

"If a believer marries a person who has divorced their spouse for any other reason other than the exceptions given in scripture, God will NOT be able to bless that marriage."

Really? God will not be able to bless that marriage? Does that sound like God? That is not the God I see revealed in scripture. The Bible teaches that the God of the Old and New Covenant CAN and DOES bless anyone He chooses to bless. Does it not say that God not only blesses the just, but also the unjust?

If a believer divorces and remarries, does that believer then live in a state of perpetual adultery? What happened to the God who removes our sin as far as the east is from the west and remembers them no more? Does God violate His own Word and say every day, "You're in a state of perpetual adultery, you're in a state of perpetual adultery!" This seems to be the correct deduction from Scripture based on what Jesus said in Matthew 5. The question I want to put to you is did Jesus really say that?

Could it be that the church has got this one wrong? As we've already seen, the church does not always get it right! How many times have you had to change your views over the years? Perhaps your view might change in this arena as well as we, like the Bereans, examine Father's Word on this issue of divorce. Did Jesus really say what it sounds like He said in Matthew 5:32? I don't think so! Please don't hear me as arrogant, that's not my heart. When the church internationally believes a certain view, do you realize how frightening it is to stand up and say, "I'm sorry everybody, but you're wrong!" And please understand when we present this different understanding, it's not an attempt to be different or unique, it's to find out what the truth is. As stated earlier, the truth sets people free. That also means that wherever there is error, there is going to be bondage, and we do not need bondage in any arena of our lives. So today, you and I are going to have a Greek lesson, a history lesson, and a Hebrew lesson!

Father, we herald loudly in prayer, what you have heralded in your Word, that faith in the Person and Work of Christ makes all men new, and restores them completely to you. We believe as you have taught, that you restore the years that the locusts have eaten, and that You make beauty out of ashes. We believe that all things work together for good, even our sin in the hands of the Holy Spirit can be used for our good. You are that Great! Oh Father, can we dare to believe this to be true in the arena of divorce? Father, I believe we can. Father please guide us into truth, and guard our hearts from error as we continue this study.

THE CRITICAL GREEK TRANSLATION ERROR

In the Greek there is a word called—*apostasion*—it means "to divorce" and specifically "to divorce in writing." There is another Greek word—*apoluo*—which CAN mean to divorce, but in an abundance of its usage in the Bible it translates—"to release or to put away!" A lot of Bible teachers and especially our translations use these words interchangeably and translate them "divorce." My question to you is this: what if we didn't use the words interchangeably? What if we translated them technically according to their primary root meaning? Would that change our understanding?

Let's look at the key passages in the New Testament that teach on divorce. First, let's look at Matthew 5:31-2. Here in this passage we're going to find both words—*apostasion*—to divorce in writing; and *apoluo*—to put away. Both words are used in this section but both are translated divorce. Ponder that with me. Why would Jesus use two different words in one section to refer to the same issue? Could it be that He had a different emphasis He wanted to address? Note that in the New American Standard Matthew 5:31 translates this way: "Whoever divorces (*apoluo*) his wife let him give her a certificate of divorce (*apostasion*)." Look at what would happen if we translated the words according to their root meaning: "Whoever puts away his wife, let him give her a certificate of divorce." Do you see how this changes the meaning of the verse? Now it becomes very clear that if a man sends away his wife and chooses to not live with her anymore, he is to write her a bill of divorce. Why? So that it is clear to all parties that the marriage has been dissolved and the wife is now single.

Now let's go to verse 32 of Matthew 5. The New American translates: "Every one of you who divorces (*apoluo*) his wife except for the cause of adultery makes her commit adultery and whoever marries a divorced (*apoluo*) woman commits adultery." Notice above that the word for divorce (*apostasion*) is not found in this verse. Instead we find the word "put away" (*apoluo*) and if we translate it according to its root meaning, note that it perfectly fits the above understanding of verse 31. "Every one of you who puts away his wife (*apoluo*) except for the cause of adultery, makes her commit adultery. And whoever marries a 'put away' woman commits adultery."

COULD WE HAVE MISUNDERSTOOD WHAT JESUS SAID?

Now let's put it together—you see what Jesus is saying, my friends? If a woman is "put away" (in other words the husband says, "I have had enough! Get OUT, we're done!" If a husband (or wife) does that, they should also give a bill of divorce and officially end the marriage. But what if a man were to put away his wife without giving her the bill of divorce? Jesus says in that instance such a man is "causing" her to commit adultery. Why? Because women did not work in that culture. Women in that day were dependent on their families for support. If you put away your wife without giving her a bill of divorce, she is in actuality still married and unable to remarry. In such an instance, the only means for her survival is to live with another man in an adulterous situation or to become a prostitute. In other words, she is going to have to commit adultery. Do we have a record of such a thing? We just might in John chapter 4, where we find the account of the Samaritan woman. She was living with a man who was not her husband, and it is very probable based on the context of having had several husbands that she had been put away without a divorce certificate. Matthew 5:32 then is pretty clear—"whoever marries a 'put away' woman commits adultery." Why? Because she was never given a bill of divorce. Legally, she is still married. That's why it is causing her to commit adultery because she has been placed into a situation by her husband where she is unable to get remarried.

Now some Bible scholars might say, "What about Mark 10?" In Mark 10 it says, "Whoever divorces his spouse and marries another commits adultery." That seems very concise and clear. Anytime a man gets divorced and remarries, he is committing adultery. But what are the Greek words being used here? Again, the word here is not *apostasion* (divorce in writing)! The word is *apoluo*. When it is translated accordingly it becomes very clear what Jesus was saying. Whoever "puts away" their spouse and marries another commits adultery. Why? Again, because there has never been a legal divorce and the original couple is still legally married. Therefore, the new marriage is in actuality an adulterous state because the former marriage is not really former. Now that is the Greek emphasis, what about the history?

JESUS CONDEMNED ABANDONMENT, NOT DIVORCE

It is my conviction that in ancient Israel, men were putting away their wives without giving them a bill of divorce and sentencing their wives to commit adultery in order to survive. How do we know that? From the very best history book we have—the Bible. We have already seen it implied from Matthew 5:31-32 and Mark 10, that men, who had all the rights in that culture, were "putting away" their wives without giving them a certificate of divorce. Jesus made it clear in Matthew 5 that this was causing the women to commit adultery as they had no viable means of support. In Matthew 19, Jesus confronted this practice by informing such men that they too were committing adultery. Note in verse 3 that the Pharisees have come to test Jesus with this question. "Is it lawful for a man to divorce his wife for any reason?" Once again, we need to go to the Greek words for help. When we do, we find that the word is not *apostasion* (divorce), but once again, as it consistently is in the New Testament, *apoluo*—to put or send away. The Pharisees were in actuality asking: "Is it lawful for a man to put away his wife for any reason at all?" Let me illustrate it for you: I've been married to Janet for thirty-three years. She BURNS my toast and I decide that she has burned my toast once too often! That's it. I'm putting you away, Janet! And I cast her out of the house with no viable means of support. Now, since I am male in that culture, I have all the rights! So, I decide to go get remarried. In that culture she can't work. She has to go live with a man or sell herself in order to survive.

Now, in ancient Israel, there were two schools of Rabbinical thought. One was the conservative Shamai school which advocated divorce/putting away only for serious issues like adultery. The other Rabbinical school was the Hillel or liberal school, which advocated divorce or putting away for any reason at all. Of course among men, the Hillel school was the preferred school to follow. If your wife spent too much money, or gained a few pounds, or argued with you for any reason, then just put her away and go get another wife. This was the heart behind what the Pharisees were asking. "So is it okay for us to put away (*apoluo*) our wife for any reason at all?" What did Jesus answer? Are you familiar with Matthew 19? Let me paraphrase what He said, "No, my people, that's not how it was supposed to be. Did you not hear when God designed this thing called marriage? He said the two of you shall become one flesh; and what

God joins together let no man ever separate." In response, those quick thinking Pharisees then asked,

"Then why did Moses command to give a bill of divorce (*apostasion*)?"

Did you hear that? In Deuteronomy 24:1, God commanded that a bill of divorce be given when a woman is put away. He stated that it was not enough just to send your wife away, you must send her away with a bill of divorce so that (verse 2) she can be married to another man. Did you see that? Not only did God command a bill of divorce to be given, he commanded that in a context with no qualifiers. He did not say only if you are married to an unbeliever. He did not say only if your spouse commits adultery. He just said if a marriage breaks up, and couples are going to go their separate ways, make sure that the marriage is completely dissolved with a certificate of divorce, so that a remarriage can occur. Now stay with me because this is very important. The Pharisees have asked if it is alright for them to "put away" their wives for any reason. Jesus in response, has told them that from the beginning this was not what God intended for marriage. God intended marriage to last for life. Quickly, they jumped in and questioned, and rightly so, "Why, then, did God command divorce?" Jesus answered, "Because of the hardness of your hearts." God commanded for there to be divorce because man's heart can be so vile and wicked that he would put away his wife when she had no means of support, thereby forcing her into adultery. The gracious and loving command from the heart of

God was to command divorce in order to protect the woman from such a hard-hearted husband. Please understand; the hard heart that Jesus was condemning in this context was not the hard heart that people have when they divorce, though that does happen. I trust you know that when people get divorced they very often have hard hearts? What he was condemning was the hard heart that would put away a woman with no resources for her own survival, forcing her to commit adultery by living with a man or becoming a prostitute.

But Jesus was not finished. When they began their examination, the Pharisees had no idea they were going to be cross-examined by the Judge of all judges Himself. Having answered their question, He then gives them more than they asked for. In verse 9 of Matthew 19, He states, "Whoever divorces his wife and marries another commits adultery." Let's be like the Bereans here and dig a little. When we do, we find that the word Jesus chose is not "divorce" (*apostasion*), but "put away" (*apoluo*). It should be translated like this: "Whoever puts away his wife and marries another commits adultery." On what grounds can Jesus make this declaration? Because they violated the command they just used in Deuteronomy 24. When they put away their wives, because of their hard hearts, they did not grant those wives a divorce. So not only are the wives still married to those men, and unable to remarry without committing adultery, those men are also still married to their original wives. This means that when they remarry, they are committing adultery as well. May I be so bold as to put an interpretative paraphrase into this context? In essence, Jesus declared,

> "You're religious little stinkers; you are putting away your wives and moving on with your lives and marrying others—all because you are a man and you have all the rights. Well, you are dead wrong! Putting away your wife forces your wife to commit adultery in order to survive. In marrying another, you commit adultery because you never released your wife with a certificate of divorce."

In the event of a marriage collapse—as there will be in our fallen world, God is crystal clear in His Word: before the couple parts ways, there must be a certificate of divorce provided. This not only officially ends the marriage, but it frees both parties to remarry. As Deuteronomy 24:2 states in distinct simplicity, "and she leaves his house and goes and becomes another man's wife." She gets remarried and God Himself condones the remarriage.

While I was studying this issue of "putting away" versus divorce many years ago, I happened to be reading a copy of *The Advocate*, our local newspaper in Baton Rouge. On page 17A was an article detailing that the ancient practice of "putting away" has been revived in modern Israel. In Israel today, men are putting away their wives in a practice called "anchoring" without giving them a bill of divorce. This practice leaves the women in a condition called "*agronaut*", meaning they are unable to marry again or to bear children within the faith. They are freed from these restrictions only when the husbands sign a divorce petition, called a "*get*." These men, just like in days of old, often get remarried and live a wonderful new life with their new families while their wives are held in bondage to their original marriage. In the article it tells of a Rabbi, who under the authority of the Rabbinical Court in Israel, hunts down these hard-hearted men. When he finds them he uses any means possible to get these men to sign a divorce certificate so their wives can be free to move on with their lives and remarry.

Father, what a revelation we have seen today, but it was not a pleasant one to be sure. Men's hearts can be so hard, that they would put their wives in states of adultery rather than do the loving thing and set them free with a certificate of divorce. Thank you for the revelation of grace in your Word, that would not only allow, but command a divorce so that people can be provided a second chance to live their lives in freedom and love. Thank you for opening our eyes to the truth of Your Word and the love that you have for us.

6

"GOD HATES DIVORCE" DOESN'T MEAN WHAT YOU THINK IT DOES

As I have presented this teaching over the years, there has been a single unified cry from the hearers from a verse in the Old Testament which, at first glance, really seems to stand against and negate what I've said here. The verse is Malachi 2:16. "For the Lord, the God of Israel, says that He hates divorce."

So there you have it, and what sounded like good teaching goes up in smoke. GOD HATES DIVORCE! I would agree, wouldn't you? God hates divorce just like He hates lying, just like He hates gossip, just like He hates the proud, arrogant spirit in Proverbs 6. God hates anything that goes against His perfect desire for us. But is that really what Malachi said? Just as we saw in the New Testament passages that the Greek language gave us greater insight into what was being said, so now in the Old Testament there are Hebrew words that will aid our understanding of what God was really saying.

The first word we need to learn is the Hebrew word, "*keryithuwth*", which means "to cut or to divorce in writing." There is another Hebrew word, "*shalach*" which can also mean "to divorce." There are, in fact, three times in the Old Testament where it is translated as "divorce." But in literally hundreds of other usages in the Old Testament it is translated "to send away."

Now here's the key. The word "*keryithuwth*" or "divorce in writing" is NOT the word that is found in Malachi 2:16! Instead the word we find there is "*shalach*"—"putting away"! Did you see it my friend? The thing that God hates, with so much hatred that He heralds it loudly and specifically for all to hear is PUTTING AWAY! Why does He hate it so much? Because it is such an ugly thing to do to a woman! The loving and kind thing would be, if you despise your wife so much that you don't want to be married to her anymore, to give her a bill of divorce and set her free just like God commanded in His Word from Deuteronomy 24:1-2! Let her have the opportunity to go and remarry. Hard-hearted men do not have the right to sentence their wives to singleness and oppression.

7

GOD HIMSELF IS A DIVORCEE

Having completed our brief Greek, history, and Hebrew lesson, what are we to say in terms of what Father's Word has declared?

First and foremost, divorce is not the unpardonable sin many have made it out to be! God Himself divorced his bride… how could divorce be a sin if God, who is perfect and sinless, issued a certificate of Divorce to Israel? Jeremiah 3:8 is perfectly clear: He gave Israel a bill of divorce and then He sent her away.

Our Father, in an effort to extend grace to his kids, even went so far as to command complete divorce so that remarriage can occur. If you are divorced, I believe it's clear from what we've seen today, that you are free to remarry, even if the reasons for your divorce are not the ones historically accepted by the church. If you are married to an unbeliever and the unbeliever leaves, you are called to peace and free to remarry. If your spouse commits adultery, though God's ideal would be for forgiveness and restoration, you likewise are free to divorce and remarry. And in accordance with Deuteronomy 24, if you find that there are other "deal breakers" for your marriage, you too are free to divorce and remarry.

Please know however, that God DOES indeed hate divorce. He hates divorce like He hates everything that is less than His ideal and original intent for His beloved creation. Affirm that it is never God's ideal to sin, but let it be known that there is forgiveness and restoration for the sin of divorce just like there is forgiveness and restoration for all other sins.

I would also share with you that divorce is NEVER to be the first option. God is very concerned about marriage because marriage pictures our relationship with Jesus. Here at Grace Life Fellowship, we NEVER counsel people to get divorced. That's not our job! Grace Life Fellowship always counsels for forgiveness and restoration, but at the same time, we teach from the Scripture that God allows divorce and remarriage. We would affirm to you that you have the freedom to do that, but we would also tell you PLEASE make that the last option. Strive for restoration. Restoration is ALWAYS the heart of God. After all, that was the basis for sending His Son for us... to restore that which was lost.

As we consider remarriage, there is an important point that I need to make: God hates adultery.

COULD WE HAVE MISUNDERSTOOD WHAT JESUS SAID? 51

One can't work with couples embroiled in troubled relationships without encountering aspects of adultery. Since God is serious about this, we in the church must take adultery seriously as well.

As long as a marriage relationship exists, neither partner is to entertain a physical relationship—or even a vicarious emotional relationship—outside the marriage. Remember the words of Paul in Romans 2: to commit adultery in the heart or mind is to be guilty of committing the act itself.

Over the years my staff and I have encountered people who wanted a divorce because they were already in a physical or emotional relationship with someone other than their spouse. By securing a divorce, they reasoned this would afford them the freedom to marry their newfound love. Make no mistake though: People of this mindset and disposition are committing adultery and trying to absolve themselves of their sin via divorce.

Scripture is very clear. God hates adultery.

In situations such as these, and when repentance hasn't occurred, my staff and I pursue church discipline. By introducing measures designed to guide a person to genuine repentance, our tough love and ongoing engagement is intended to create an honest and redemptive atmosphere for repentance, healing, and hope. Pursuing a divorce to legitimize adultery is sin. Every time.

Just as love will discipline a child that continues to run into the street and place themselves in harm's way, the church must lovingly discipline those who pursue sinful paths and place themselves in harm's way. Divorce is an option for marriages that are broken, not as a means of escape so one can "legitimately" pursue an adulterous relationship.

Marriage, divorce, and remarriage are complex. Add to the mix of relationship the variety of ways sinful flesh can try to avoid the hard labor of love and anything can occur. We must engage people at their point of need. We must be careful to honor God. And while it should go without saying, to state the obvious: We must skillfully rely upon the Holy Spirit for wisdom.

As my buddy who wrote the foreword to this book has written, "There must be a place where shame meets grace—and I can be in that place."

And what about separation? It's a valid issue in the New Testament and it may be pursued by you but it should be pursued only with a heart that longs for and seeks forgiveness and restoration. Marriage is tough stuff! May I share with you some words that really nail this? "To have and to hold from this day forward; for better, for worse, for richer, for poorer, in sickness, in health, to love and to cherish 'til death do us part."

As Chuck Swindoll so eloquently says, "Are any words more tenderly holy than those of the marriage ceremony? And is there any union more deep, and more joyous than that of a man and a woman becoming one flesh? God designed marriage to be a delightfully intimate partnership: a union of warm innocence. He creates beauty in all things and marriage is His masterpiece in the realm of relationships. But, just as the beauty of His holiness breathes things to life, so sin mars ALL with its cold death touch. Like a butterfly's exuberant flight seared by a merciless sun, marriages are withered by sin. The one flesh is rent into two shredded and bleeding individuals. Some mask the pain of their separateness by retaining the form of a marriage, living lives of quiet desperation as they plow through their days. Others become angry, pounding out their differences through psychological or physical abuse; with howling hands they beat their spouses into submission: with brutal words they bludgeon them self-esteemless. Separation offers an escape, a rest from a marriage gone bad, but a house divided cannot stand, and those who try to mend the broken pieces of their lives apart from each other seldom find the solution that is needed to reunite because they are going to do it on their own. At the last, divorce hisses in confusion, the serpent invades the garden and drives the relationship into dust."

Oh my friend, marriage is tough stuff! Marriage is not for cowards! Marriage is for those who have tenacity. And may I tell you that marriage is abnormal? You believe that, don't you? I hope you do! If you went to kindergarten, you know that in a natural world—one plus one equals two. God is asking us to do one plus one equals one! That's weird! If you think one plus one equals one, your checkbook is going to be in some major trouble! You are going to bounce some checks! I'm telling you, dear one, that one plus one becoming one does not work in the natural realm! The only way one plus one equals one, is if we have one plus one plus ONE that will equal one! You will NEVER pull this thing off apart from God.

I want to leave you with a final word. We need to spot-check our attitudes towards the divorced. Too often we treat these hurting brothers and sisters as if they had committed the unpardonable sin. We cut them off from ministry and social circles they once enjoyed. We leave them to grieve their losses and piece together their lives alone. When we find ourselves in their company we frequently look for the nearest exit. Remember, divorce is forgivable and as Christians we are to be a forgiving people; people who console and reconcile, not condemn and chastise. Divorced Christians need our love, they need our embrace, they need our encouragement, they need our friendship. Let's not forsake them! Let's accept them with open, forgiving arms. That's how Jesus treats divorced people!

Saints, I threw a lot at you today, I'm not asking you to believe it; I'm asking you to study it and see if these things are not true! Jesus wasn't saying that people are in a state of perpetual adultery if they get remarried. That's only true if you put away your spouse without divorcing them. There's been way too much error and way too much bondage. We need to start standing for truth and minister the freedom, grace, forgiveness, and restoration that the Lord Jesus Christ secured and offers to ALL who put their faith in Him.

Father, I pray for your people. It's very frightening, Father, to go contrary to what so many believe and what Your church has taught for centuries. But Your Word, I think, is pretty clear; and if it's clear, then we need to embrace it no matter what the consequences. We are not here to defend our reputation; we are not here to be unique and different; we are here to herald truth; truth that sets us free. Because as Your Word says, 'it was for freedom that Christ died to make us free'. And in Christ, Father, the bondage needs to end. Divorce is no different from any other sin and sometimes people experience divorce innocently because the other spouse refuses to repent and we need to allow them the freedom that Your Word does—to remarry and not be sentenced for the rest of their lives to singleness, and not be sentenced to burn with passion. Let it be! In Jesus name. Amen.

A NOTE TO CHURCH LEADERS

It has been said that the church is the only entity that shoots its own wounded. This is a travesty and a tragedy. I find it a powerful statement that when God became flesh the very first thing observed by man was that God in the flesh was full of grace and truth. Those two must go hand in hand. We must ever be the ones who are in search of truth because it is the truth that sets men free. If that is true, and I believe it is, the reverse is also true. Lies produce bondage. There has been far too much bondage in the church through a failure to search out the truth in this area and a failure to show grace to those who so desperately need it. My dear fellow shepherd, I would encourage you to do your own study in this area and see if what has been shared is true. If it is true, then herald it to others that they might receive the forgiveness and restoration that is their birthright in Jesus Christ.

A NOTE TO READERS CONSIDERING DIVORCE

I believe there are times when a marriage has to end. The human heart can be so full of ill intent that we can do irreparable damage to each other. At the same time, the human heart is so fragile, that it cannot bear to be wounded in such great fashion. Put simply, God allows divorce. We are all living in a world that we were never designed to live in. This is not Eden, and many, many people are mortally wounded emotionally by the wounds they have received in a marriage gone bad.

However, pain and suffering are never the end of the story with God. He is a Redeemer. He is one who restores. He can bring beauty out of ashes. He can restore the years that the locusts have eaten. He can resurrect from the dead those that have been mortally wounded. He is so good and so powerful that He can make ALL things to work together for good. Did you notice that He said "ALL THINGS"? I am fully persuaded that incredible reality applies even to our sin. God can take our sin and even the sins of those who have wounded us so badly, and bring good consequences out of it.

Why do I share this? Because it is my conviction that many people bail out of a marriage before fully giving God the opportunity to restore the marriage. Please know, that restoration will not be easy. You will have to work through many hurtful situations that have occurred and many murderous words that have been spoken. I have often referred to this process as going through surgery without anesthesia but the surgery can occur and the marriage can be healed. Please seek quality Christian counseling before signing on the dotted line that spells death to your marriage. Remember, with God all things are possible.

A NOTE TO DIVORCED READERS

It is time. This is your day. You have carried the guilt and the shame of your divorce for too long and it is indeed time for you to embrace the forgiveness and restoration that God has provided for you at the cross of His Son. You are forgiven! You are loved! You are free! You are not a second class citizen in the kingdom of God! You are certainly NOT in a state of perpetual adultery. God recognizes your divorce. If it was sinfully pursued, you are forgiven. If you were the innocent party, you are called to peace. If you are remarried, know that God affirms your marriage and blesses it in the blessed name of Jesus. Hold your head high as a child of God and know that He loves you and that He is pleased with you and proud to call you His child, His trophy of grace.

Now, if you are in a church that continues to guilt and shame you with what has been forever erased at the cross, I need to offer you a little pastoral counsel in the form of a question. Why are you still in that church? With all the love I can muster, get out of there as fast as you can and find an assembly that not only proclaims the grace of God in Christ, but practices it! It may take you a while, but such churches do exist and they will welcome you as the saint you are through your faith in the FINISHED work of Christ. In such a church, you will be able to become the functioning member of the body of Christ that He re-created you to be. This is my hope and prayer for you. "Come to Me, all who are weary and heavy laden, and I will give you rest. Take My yoke upon you, and learn from Me, for I am gentle and humble in heart; and you shall find rest for your souls. For My yoke is easy, and My load is light" (Matthew 11:28-30).

ACKNOWLEDGEMENTS

I owe a debt of gratitude to Nick Kalivoda, a very gifted Bible teacher who first challenged me to dig deeper into the original languages concerning this issue.

I would also like to thank the elders of Grace Life Fellowship. They have been dear friends and fellow students of Father's Word with me for many years, and together we have sought to discover and proclaim the truth that sets men free. It is my joy to serve in the ministry with them, and call them brothers.

- Frank Friedmann

LIVING IN GRACE

Living in Grace is the Bible teaching ministry of Frank Friedmann. It exists to help men and women from all walks of life experience and express Jesus. Most Christians live with constant guilt, shame, anxiety, emptiness, and loss. Jesus Christ promises joy, rest, peace, freedom, and abundant life to ALL those who put their faith in Him.

Frank has written several books on living in grace. They're scheduled for release in 2016.

WHERE TO FIND US

Grace Life Fellowship
10210 Baringer Foreman Rd.
Baton Rouge, LA 70809

225-769-8844

For free sermons, articles, and videos visit

FrankFriedmann.com

BOOKS BY FRANK FRIEDMANN

The Impossible Christian Life

The Impossible Christian Life Self-Study

Parenting in Grace

Masturbation: What Does God Really Think?

Sex: What Every Teen Should Know

CHILDREN'S BOOKS BY FRANK FRIEDMANN

Who Am I?

I Was Wrong, But God Made Me Right

If I'm Right, Why Do I Keep Doing Wrong?

Made in the USA
Coppell, TX
09 October 2021